Checking the Weather

by Elyse Schwartz

Illustrated by Colleen Madden

PEARSON

Glenview, Illinois • Boston, Massachusetts • Chandler, Arizona
Hoboken, New Jersey

Illustrated by Colleen Madden

ISBN 13: 978-0-328-81995-9
ISBN 10:   0-328-81995-6
1 2 3 4 5 6 7 8 9 10 V0B4 18 17 16 15 14

How will we check the weather?

Mom reads the newspaper.

Dad watches TV.

Mike uses the computer.

Meg listens to the radio.

I go outside!